D1478114

Giggle Wiggle
Pregnancy Journal

BY ELIZABETH & ALEX LLUCH

WS Publishing Group
San Diego, California

GIGGLE WIGGLE PREGNANCY JOURNAL

By Elizabeth & Alex Lluch

Published by WS Publishing Group
San Diego, California 92119
Copyright © 2011 by WS Publishing Group

All rights reserved under International and Pan-American Copyright Conventions. No part of this book may be reproduced or transmitted in any form or by any means, electronic or mechanical, including photocopy, recording or by any information storage and retrieval system, without permission in writing from the publisher.

Image Credits:
Front cover image: © iStockphoto/minimil

For more information on this and many other best-selling books visit
www.WSPublishingGroup.com.
E-mail: info@WSPublishingGroup.com

ISBN 13: 978-1-936061-28-0

Printed in China

Place photo of
you during your
pregnancy here

THE HAPPY MOMMY-TO-BE

DEDICATED TO MOTHERS-TO-BE EVERYWHERE.
MAY PREGNANCY BE THE ONE OF THE MOST
SPECIAL JOURNEYS OF YOUR LIFE.

CONTENTS

CONTENTS

All About Me

"There was a place in childhood that I remember well,
And there a voice of sweetest tone bright fairy tales did tell." – Samuel Lover

MY STORY

When & where I was born: ....

Time I was born: ....

Height: .... Hair color: .... Eye color: ....

Siblings: ....

Favorite food: ....

Favorite pastime: ....

Favorite hangout: ....

Three words to describe me: ....

My earliest memory: ....

....

....

A favorite memory from childhood: ....

....

....

....

"Families are like fudge—mostly sweet with a few nuts." – Anonymous

Place a favorite photo
of you from before
your pregnancy here

A FAVORITE PHOTO OF ME

MY FAMILY TREE

Mother .... Father...

Grandmother.. Grandmother...

Grandfather .... Grandfather..

Great Grandfather .... Great Grandfather ....

Great Grandmother .... Great Grandmother ....

A favorite memory with my siblings:...

....

A favorite memory with my cousins:...

....

A favorite memory with my grandparents:..

A wonderful vacation we took as a family: ....

Family pets I had:...

One tradition in my family:...

An important holiday in my family: ....

"Life without love is like a tree without blossoms or fruit." – Kahlil Gibran

Place photo of you with
your family here

NOTHING SAYS LOVE
LIKE FAMILY

IMAGING MOTHERHOOD

The number of children I thought I would have and why: ....

....

I wanted this many boys and girls:...

Qualities that I feel will make me a great mother: ....

....

Fond memories of my own mother:...

....

....

Qualities I look for in a father to my child: ....

....

....

Baby names I have always liked: ....

....

....

The age I imagined I would have my first child: ....

"To understand a mother's love, bear your own children." – Chinese Proverb

Place photo of you and
your mother here

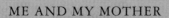

ME AND MY MOTHER

REFLECTIONS FROM THE HEART

Reflections on who or what from my childhood best prepared me to be a mother:....................

....

....

....

....

....

....

....

....

....

....

....

Date: ....

Dreaming
of a Baby

"God could not be everywhere and therefore he made mothers."
– A Jewish Proverb

VISIONS OF SUGARPLUMS

My pregnancy was planned or a surprise?...

I first began thinking about having a baby: ....

....

....

Why I wanted to have a baby: ....

....

When I imagined my life with a baby, I felt: ....

....

....

Physical traits I hope my baby will inherit from me:..

....

Traits I hope the baby will inherit from its father: ....

....

Personality characteristics I hope my baby will inherit:..

....

"Being in love shows a person who he should be." – Anton Chekov

Place photo of you or
picture of you with
your partner here

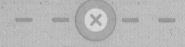

MAKING A BABY WITH LOVE

CREATING NEW LIFE

I thought it was a good time to have a baby because: ....

....

....

Challenges I expect with having a baby: ....

....

....

When I imagined being pregnant, I felt: ....

....

One thing I changed before becoming pregnant: ....

....

How I prepared for getting pregnant: ....

....

....

How long it took to get pregnant: ....

....

"Where there is love, there is life." – Gandhi

Place photo of
you before your
pregnancy here

ME BEFORE MY PREGNANCY

REFLECTIONS FROM THE HEART

Reflections on imagining pregnancy and my life with a baby:...

....

....

....

....

....

....

....

....

....

....

....

....

....

Date: ....

Wonderful News

"A baby is God's opinion that the world should go on." – Carl Sandburg

I'M EXPECTING!

I first thought I might be pregnant because: ....

....

Day and place when I first suspected: ....

How I confirmed my pregnancy: ....

Once my pregnancy was confirmed, I felt: ....

....

....

I was overjoyed because: ....

....

I was nervous because: ....

....

The first thing I did was: ....

....

....

"The sweetest sounds to mortals given; Are heard in Mother, Home, and Heaven."
— William Goldsmith Brown

Place photo from the
day you learned you
were pregnant here

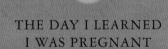

THE DAY I LEARNED
I WAS PREGNANT

FAMILY AND FRIENDS' REACTIONS

The first person I told about my pregnancy:..
....

How the first person I told reacted to the news:..
....

My partner's reaction:..
....
....

My parents' reactions:..
....
....

His parents' reactions:..
....
....

My close friends' reactions:...
....

"A grand adventure is about to begin." – Winnie the Pooh

Place photo of you
with friends and
family here

FRIENDS AND FAMILY

CELEBRATING MY BABY

What I did to celebrate my pregnancy:..

....

Where I went:..

Why I chose that location:...

....

Loved ones who joined me:..

....

Person who was most excited for me:..

....

First pregnancy or baby book I received:...

First gift I received:..

....

Memorable moments:...

....

"A baby is sunshine and moonbeams and more brightening
your world as never before." – Anonymous

Place photo from celebration of your pregnancy here

CELEBRATING THE BIG
NEWS

REFLECTIONS FROM THE HEART

Reflections on emotions I felt during the first days I learned I was pregnant: ....

....

....

....

....

....

....

....

....

....

....

....

....

Date: ....

The First
Trimester

"i carry your heart with me
(i carry it in my heart)
i am never without it
anywhere i go you go, my dear ..." – e.e. cummings

HOPING, WISHING, DREAMING

I am most looking forward to: ....
....

I am most nervous about: ....
....
....

I am most excited about: ....
....

I am least excited about: ....
....

Important people who will help me and how: ....
....

My shoulder to lean on will be: ....
....
....

"My life has been the awaiting of you.
Your footfall was my own heart's beat." – Paul Valery

Place photo of you from
the 1st month here

MY 1ST MONTH

FIRST DOCTOR'S VISIT

Date & location: ....

Before my first appointment, I felt:...

....

My doctor:...

I chose my doctor because:...

....

Procedure performed: ....

Baby's progress: ....

....

After my appointment, I felt: ....

....

Thing I need to keep in mind:...

....

Notes: ....

....

"Life is magic, the way nature works seems to be quite magical." – Jonas Salk

Place memento from your first appointment here

MEMENTO FROM MY FIRST
APPOINTMENT

PEA IN A POD

During the first weeks, I felt:...

....

....

My mood:..

My energy: ....

My skin: ....

My hair: ....

My body: ....

Any sickness?: ....

My appetite has been: ....

Strangest food I crave:...

My new favorite food: ....

Food I can't touch!:...

Staples of my pregnancy diet: ....

....

"We live only to discover beauty. All else is a form of waiting." – Kahlil Gibran

Place photo of you from
the 2nd month here

MY 2ND MONTH

FIRST GLIMPSES

Before my ultrasound I felt:..

....

The ultrasound revealed:..

....

My reaction when I first saw the baby:...

....

My reaction when I heard the heartbeat:..

....

My partner's reactions:..

....

Any surprises?:...

....

After the scan, I felt:..

....

"There are two things in life for which we are never fully prepared,
and that is twins." – Josh Billings

Place a photo from the
ultrasound scan here

THE ULTRASOUND

MY PROGRESS

My first trimester weight: ....

When I first started to show: ....

....

Biggest change in my body: ....

....

Most significant change in my life: ....

....

....

The hardest thing to get used to: ....

....

....

What I am doing to stay healthy: ....

....

....

"Better keep yourself clean and bright; you are the window through which you must see the world." – George Bernard Shaw

Place photo of you from the 3rd month here

MY 3RD MONTH

MY FIRST TRIMESTER, LOOKING BACK

Most memorable day: ....
....

Most memorable moment: ....
....

Most unexpected occurrence: ....

Most emotional moment: ....
....

Funniest moment: ....
....

My favorite part about being a new pregnant mom: ....
....

A special moment my partner and I shared: ....
....
....

"Of all music that reaches farthest into heaven,
is the beating of a loving heart." – Henry Ward Beecher

Place a special
photo from your first
trimester here

FAVORITE PICTURE FROM
MY FIRST TRIMESTER

REFLECTIONS FROM THE HEART

Reflections on the first trimester: ....
....
....
....
....
....
....
....
....
....
....
....
....

Date: ....

The Second Trimester

"I am beginning to learn that it is the sweet, simple
things of life which are the real ones after all." – Laura Ingalls Wilder

LEARNING & GROWING

This trimester, I am hoping: ....
....

I am most looking forward to: ....
....

I am most nervous about: ....
....

I am most excited about: ....
....
....

I am least excited about: ....
....
....

Something amazing I've learned so far: ....
....
....

"Wherever you go, go with all your heart." – Confucius

Place photo of you from
the 4th month here

MY 4TH MONTH

BUN IN THE OVEN

My mood: ....

....

My energy: ....

....

My cravings: ....

....

My back: ....

....

My feet: ....

....

The first time I felt the baby kick: ....

When the baby moved, I felt: ....

Describe the sensation: ....

First person I let feel the baby moving: ....

His or her reaction: ....

"You are my honey, honeysuckle, I am the bee." – Albert H. Fitz

Place photo of you from
the 5th month here

MY 5TH MONTH

BELLY BOUTIQUE

The first day I wore maternity clothes was: ....
....

What I wore: ....
....

My favorite maternity store: ....
....

My favorite maternity designers: ....
....

Outfit that makes me feel cute: ....
....

Most comfortable outfit: ....
....

Least comfortable article of clothing: ....
....

Something I can no longer wear that I miss: ....

"We can do no great things; only small things with great love." – Mother Teresa

Place photo of you
in your favorite
maternity outfit here

MY MATERNITY STYLE

AN IMPORTANT CHECKUP

I decided to have or not to have a fetal anomaly ultrasound because: ....

....

Before the test, I felt: ....

....

Questions I had for my doctor: ....

....

My worries: ....

....

Afterward, I felt: ....

....

Baby's features I could see on the monitor: ....

....

Notes: ....

....

"Whenever a woman gives birth to a child, she remembers the hard work no more, for the joy
that a child has been born into the world." – John 16:21

Place photo of you from
a day you felt great here

A DAY I FELT GREAT

PINK OR BLUE?

My partner and I decided we did or did not want to know the baby's sex because: ....

....

....

....

The decision was:...

I predicted the sex to be:..

My partner predicted the sex to be:...

Who was correct?: ....

Any surprises?:..

....

....

....

Our reactions to learning the baby's sex were: ..:..

....

....

"I have found the one whom my soul loves." – Song of Solomon 3:4

Place memento from
when you found out
the sex of your baby

GIRL OR BOY?

MY PROGRESS

My second trimester weight:...Waist:...........................

Most significant change in my life: ....

....

....

The hardest thing to get used to:..

....

....

Biggest change in my body:...

....

....

Biggest change in the baby:...

....

....

Suggestions my doctor had for me: ....

"My mother taught me underneath a tree, And sitting down before the heat of day,
She took me on her lap and kissed me …" –William Blake

Place photo of you from
the 6th month here

MY 6TH MONTH

MY SECOND TRIMESTER, LOOKING BACK

One of the best days I had:...

....

One of the toughest days I had: ....

....

A funny memory this trimester:..

....

A day my partner and I really bonded:..

....

My favorite part about this trimester: ....

....

....

....

Most unexpected occurrence this trimester: ....

....

....

"Be intent upon the perfection of the present day." – William Law

Place a special photo
from the second
trimester here

A FAVORITE PICTURE FROM MY
SECOND TRIMESTER

REFLECTIONS FROM THE HEART

Reflections on the second trimester:..

....

....

....

....

....

....

....

....

....

....

....

....

....

....

Date: ....

The Third Trimester

"A baby's feet, like sea-shells pink Might tempt, should heaven see meet
An angel's lips to kiss, we think A baby's feet."
– Algernon Charles Swinburne

THE HOME STRETCH

My wishes for my last trimester include:..
....

I am most looking forward to: ....
....

I am most nervous about:..
....

I am most excited about: ....
....

I am least excited:...
....

I think the biggest change in the final trimester will be:...
....

How I plan to relax before my due date: ....
....

"Life is always a rich and steady time when you are waiting for
something to happen or to hatch." – E.B. White, *Charlotte's Web*

Place photo of you from
the 7th month here

MY 7TH MONTH

READY TO POP

How my body continues to change: ....
....
....
....
....
....

My mood: ....
....

My energy: ....
....

My appetite: ....
....

My cravings: ....
....

"The best and most beautiful things in the world cannot be seen or even touched.
They must be felt with the heart." – Helen Keller

Place photo of you from
the 8th month here

MY 8TH MONTH

MY BIRTH PLAN

I have selected the following birthing method: ....

Who helped me create my birth plan?: ....
....

The things that are most important to me with the birth plan: ....
....

Where I will give birth: ....
....

People who will be present at the birth: ....
....

The atmosphere I want to create: ....
....

My hopes for my delivery: ....
....
....

"You are the nectar, the hummingbird, the clover.
You are the bloom, the bee, the OerHoverer. You are the child, the bond and the mother.
You are the Love, the Beloved, the Lover." – Saiom Shriver

Place a copy of your
birth plan here

MY BIRTH PLAN

OUR PROGRESS

My weight:.. Waist:........................

My baby's features that I can clearly see: ....

....

....

Baby's movement?:..

....

....

Baby's hiccups?:..

....

....

Any early contractions?:...

....

....

The most exciting new change:..

....

"Love is trembling happiness." – Kahlil Gibran

Place photo of you from
the 9th month here

MY 9TH MONTH

REFLECTIONS FROM THE HEART

Reflections on the third trimester: ....

....

....

....

....

....

....

....

....

....

....

....

....

....

Date: ....

Planning for Baby

"If I had a flower for every time I thought of you,
I could walk in my garden forever." – Alfred Lord Tennyson

TAKING CARE OF ME

Ways I'm pampering myself: ....
....

A special treat was: ....
....

What I'm learning in prenatal or parenting class: ....
....

Most surprising thing I learned: ....
....

Yoga or other exercise I'm doing: ....
....
....

How my partner is helping me: ....
....
....

"The consciousness of loving and being loved brings a warmth and richness to life that
nothing else can bring." – Oscar Wilde

Place photo of you
being pampered here

BEING PAMPERED

MY PERFECT NURSERY

My nursery's theme:...

Colors I chose: ....

Why I chose these colors:...

....

Furniture & decorations I love: ....

....

Where I shopped: ....

....

Baby brands I love:...

....

My favorite part of my baby's room:...

....

The most fun part of designing the nursery: ....

....

"Where fall the tears of love the rose appears, And where the ground is bright with
friendship's tears, Forget-me-not, and violets, heavenly blue, Spring glittering with the
cheerful drops like dew." – William Cullen Bryant

Place photo of
nursery here

THE BABY'S NURSERY

ALL FOR YOU, MY CHILD

Favorite toy I chose for my baby: ....

Favorite outfit:...

Favorite shoes: ....

Favorite blanket:..

Favorite bath toy: ....

Favorite piece of furniture:...

Things on my wishlist:..

....

....

Gifts I received for the nursery:..

....

....

Friends and relatives who are spoiling me the most:...

....

"Sweet babe, in thy face Soft desires I can trace, Secret joys and secret smiles,
Little pretty infant wiles." – William Blake

Place photo of baby
toys or clothes here

MY BABY'S BEAUTIFUL THINGS

THE SHOWER

My baby shower was held at: ....

Date: ....

Hostess: ....

Theme: ....

Favors: ....

Special friends who attended: ....

....

Favorite gifts: ....

....

Games we played: ....

....

....

Funniest moment: ....

....

"Demonstrations of love are small, compared with the great thing that is back of them." – Kahlil Gibran

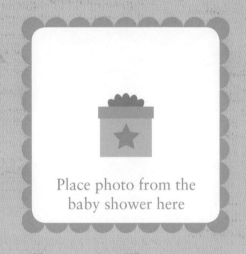

Place photo from the
baby shower here

THE BABY SHOWER

LOVE, IN A NAME

Favorite boys' names and their meanings: ....

....

Favorite girls' names and their meanings: ....

....

Family names we considered: ....

....

My partner and I narrowed it down to: ....

....

Why we love these names: ....

....

Favorite middle names: ....

....

Favorite nicknames: ....

....

"'I have no name; I am but two days old.'
What shall I call thee? I happy am, Joy is my name.'" – William Blake

Place a list of favorite baby names here

OUR FAVORITE NAMES

WAITING PATIENTLY

Last-minute preparations before the baby comes: ....

....

Days before the delivery, I am feeling: ....

....

My expectations for labor include: ....

....

I am excited about: ....

....

I am anxious about: ....

....

I am scared about:..

....

My partner feels:..

....

"Look! how he laughs and stretches out his arms, And opens wide his blue eyes upon thine, To hail his father; while his little form, Flutters as winged with joy. Talk not of pain! The childless cherubs well might envy thee, The pleasures of a parent." – Lord Byron

Place photo from the
final days of your
pregnancy here

THE LAST DAYS OF MY
PREGNANCY

REFLECTIONS FROM THE HEART

Reflections on planning for the baby's arrival: ....
....
....
....
....
....
....
....
....
....
....
....
....
....

Date: ....

Welcoming New Life

"The moment a child is born, the mother is also born.
She never existed before. The woman existed, but the mother, never.
A mother is something absolutely new."
– Bhagwan Shree Rajneesh

SPECIAL DELIVERY

When and where I felt the first contraction:...

....

I went into labor, date & time:..

Who was with me?:..

Their reaction:...

....

When I knew it was time, I felt:...

....

I was in labor for ....hours and .... minutes.

My baby was born on:.. at: ....

Loved ones present at the birth: ....

....

Memorable moment or turning point during labor:...

....

*"A woman has two smiles that an angel might envy, the smile that accepts a
lover before words are uttered, and the smile that lights on the first born babe,
and assures it of a mother's love." – Thomas C. Haliburton*

Place photo of your
newborn baby here

MY BABY'S NEWBORN PHOTO

WELCOME, BABY!

Boy or girl?: ....

My birth experience was: ....

....

What I was thinking during labor: ....

....

Immediately after the birth, I felt: ....

....

....

My first thought when I held my new baby: ....

....

....

My partner's reaction to holding the baby for the first time:................................

....

....

"There is no friendship, no love,
like that of the parent for the child." – Henry Ward Beecher

Place photo of you
and/or your partner
holding the baby here

HOLDING MY PRECIOUS BABY

MY PERFECT ANGEL

My baby's full name:..

Birth date:..

My baby's weight:...

Length:...

Hair:..

Eye color:..

Disposition:...

Who my baby most resembles and why:...

....

....

The first people I called after the birth:..

....

....

Their reactions to the good news:...

....

"When they placed you in my arms, you slipped into my heart." – Anonymous

Place baby
announcement or
picture of baby here

YOU'VE ARRIVED!

REFLECTIONS FROM THE HEART

✕

Reflections from the birth and welcoming my baby into the world: ....

....

....

....

....

....

....

....

....

....

....

....

....

....

Date: ....

✕

Bringing Home Baby

"Where your pleasure is, there is your treasure; where your treasure is, there is your heart; where your heart is, there is your happiness." – Saint Augustine

HOME SWEET HOME

Date I brought the baby home: ....

Coming home, I felt: ....

....

....

My partner felt: ....

....

....

Our first night at home was: ....

....

....

Reactions from siblings or pets: ....

....

....

....

"A baby in the house is a well-spring of pleasure, a messenger of peace and love,
a resting place for innocence on earth, a link between angels and men."
– Martin Fraquhar Tupper

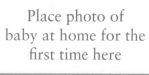

Place photo of
baby at home for the
first time here

AT HOME WITH BABY

SPECIAL VISITORS

People who came to see me and the baby: ....

....

Friends who sent congratulations: ....

....

Favorite gifts the baby and I received: ....

....

Family and friends who helped me most: ....

....

Most memorable moment: ....

....

....

Funniest moment: ....

....

....

"A woman can learn a lot from holding a new baby. It is life beginning again
— sweet possibilities! No problem in the world is big enough to be remembered."
– Susan McOmber

Place notes, cards, and congratulations here

NOTES, CARDS, AND
CONGRATULATIONS

BABY'S FIRSTS

First outfit: ....

First feeding: ....

First nap: ....

First bath: ....

....

First diaper change: ....

....

First big cry: ....

....

First silly sound: ....

....

First funny face: ....

....

"When the first baby laughed for the first time, the laugh broke into a thousand pieces
and they all went skipping about, and that was the beginning of fairies."
– James Matthew Barrie

Place photo from one
of baby's firsts here

ONE OF BABY'S FIRSTS

MY WELL-BEING

How it feels to be a mother:..

....

Now that pregnancy is over, I feel:..

....

How my body is recovering:..

....

My joys:..

....

My worries:...

....

My emotional state:...

....

Reflections on the pregnancy journey:...

....

"Doubt the stars are fire; Doubt the sun doth move; Doubt truth to be a liar;
But never doubt I love." – William Shakespeare

Place photo of you with
your baby here

ME AND MY CHILD

DEAR LITTLE ONE ... A LETTER TO MY BABY

Dear Baby, ...

....

....

....

....

....

....

....

....

....

....

....

....

....

Date: ....